Th

Amazing
Facts
for
Kids
of All Ages

Zymurgy Publishing

Zymurgy Publishing
The moral rights of author
Martin Ellis/Zymurgy
Publishing have been asserted.

A CIP catalogue record for this book is available from
the British library.

Printed & bound by CPI Group (UK) Ltd, Croydon
ISBN 978 1903506 39 4
Published by Zymurgy Publishing
Newcastle upon Tyne
10 9 8 7 6 5 4 3 2 1
© Zymurgy Publishing 2014

Acknowledgements

Many thanks to Tansee Cartwright, Ann Cotterrell, Mia Edwards, Robin Edwards, Anne Ellis, Max Haughton, Ged Kielty and Philip Mills for helping with information. Zymurgy Publishing is particularly grateful for the help and support of Millie Chadwick and Dorothy Thomas.

The television programme QI has provided inspiration and some little gems of information.

Introduction

This book is full of facts. Some of them will amaze you, some will surprise you and some will start you thinking, so that you discover more about the subject. Hopefully, after reading this book you will be a cleverer person than when you started. You don't want to be a clever clogs or a clever dick because this is someone who people mock because they show off. So it is best not to show people up for not knowing what you know and to share your knowledge instead.

In this book you will learn things about your body, animals, science, history, sport and many more subjects too.

Books always start on the right hand side

The main text in a book always starts on the right hand side. This dates to back to a time in history before books were bound into paperbacks or hardbacks and pages were loose sheets tied together with ribbon. So sometimes you have a blank page on the left at the start of a book.

The word 'swims' when turned upside down will still read swims.

Paper

It is impossible to fold a sheet of paper in half more than 8 times.

It is believed that paper was invented in China 100 B.C. Before people had paper they used to write on clay bricks or tablets. In Egypt people used to write on a material made from plants and called papyrus.

It is easier to read words printed on paper than on a computer screen. Generally people read at three quarters of the speed from a computer screen than they do if they are reading from a book, newspaper or magazine.

Writing

The Japanese read from right to left. Hebrew, which is one of the world's oldest languages and is the traditional language of Jews, is also written right to left, as is Arabic.

Traditionally, the Chinese write in columns from the top to the bottom of a page, with the columns starting on the right.

So some people probably think it is strange to read from left to right!

Words and sentences

A palindrome is a phrase or sentence which reads the same backwards as forwards.

The following are palindromes.
A Toyota's a Toyota
As I pee I see Pisa
Otto sees Otto
Hannah

'NOON' is a palindrome and (when it is written in capital letters) also reads the same when it is upside down.

A sentence that contains every letter of the alphabet it called a pangram.

The best known pangram is:

The quick brown fox jumps over a lazy dog.

The Body

Around 65 % of the human body is water.

The brain uses about a quarter of the oxygen used by the body.

Blood carries oxygen and energy around the body.

Fainting is caused by not enough blood reaching the brain.

Sneezing

Sneezing clears the nose of bacteria and viruses, so it is best not to sniff and it is healthy to blow your nose.

You can't sneeze with your eyes open!

Every time you sneeze you blink. Nobody is absolutely certain why but it may be to protect our eyes from our snot.

Sneezes can leave the body at over 100 mph particles may contain 100,000 germs. The particles in a sneeze can travel 1½ metres and the bacteria can travel much further. That's why it is important to sneeze into a handkerchief.

Why is snot green?

The correct term for snot is mucus and it is usually clear or transparent. When you have a cold or infection your mucus often turns a shade of green. This happens when the immune system – the body's way of repairing or looking after itself – gets active. The immune system sends white blood cells to the infected area, and these blood cells cause the change in colour.

You can't sneeze in your sleep.

What are bogies and why are they green?

Bogies are dried-up, hardened mucus that protects the nose from dirt, dust, debris and anything else that you don't want in your nose. The green colour in bogies is due to iron created by white blood cells.

Eskimos rub their noses together when they greet each other.

Why is poo brown?

The food that we eat comes in a range of colours: red tomatoes, green peas, white fish, yellow ice cream and very occasionally blue. So why is poo brown?

The simple answer is that the brown colour is caused by dead blood cells.

Blood has a red-coloured chemical which takes oxygen around the body. When blood gets old the liver recycles the blood, but it cannot recycle the red material so it breaks it down into a yellow material and sends it to your gut. The bacteria in your gut eats the yellow material, leaving body waste material which is brown.

Babies don't have bacteria to break down the yellow material, so baby poo is yellow.

Don't worry about the dead blood cells, your body is making new blood all the time.

Why is wee sometimes almost clear and sometimes a golden yellow?

It depends on how much water you have drunk. If your wee is concentrated because you haven't drunk much water your wee will be very yellow, but if you have drunk lots it will be much clearer. However, some people find that their wee turns red if they have been eating beetroot.

Wee has been put to a number of uses in history.

In Roman times people used to wash their mouths out with wee to get sparkling, bright white teeth, Romans collected wee so that it could be used for cleaning laundry. Wee has also been used for softening leather, helping to dye clothes and as one of the ingredients for gunpowder.

What is a burp?

When you eat or drink, you also swallow air. Your stomach doesn't want this air, so the air comes back out again as a burp.

Fizzy drinks, eating or drinking too fast can make you burp.

A burp is another word for a belch... and belching is not considered to be good manners or polite! If you are going to burp, it is best to cover your mouth and apologise.

What causes hiccups?

When you breathe in, your diaphragm (a big muscle under your lungs) pulls air into your lungs. When you breathe out your diaphragm relaxes so that air comes out through your nose and mouth. Sometimes the diaphragm pulls in air in a jerky manner, so that you suck air into your throat suddenly, and when it hits your voice box your vocal cords close, producing a hiccup.

What causes the diaphragm to take in air suddenly? It can be eating too quickly, a shock, surprise or perhaps excitement.

How do you cure hiccups?

There are many different suggestions for curing hiccups. One of the most popular is to get someone to surprise or shock you.

An old method used by actors on stage is to breathe in, hold your breath for as long as you can, then push the air into your stomach. Hopefully this will stop your hiccups.

What creates a fart?

Farts, or more politely flatulence, are gases from air that we breathe mixed with gases made inside our tummies when our body breaks down food. Bacteria and chemicals break down food so that we can get the energy and goodness we need from it.

The mixture of gases in farts varies, as some gases smell more than others. The particularly smelly odour comes from hydrogen sulphide. Eggs and meat have a reputation for creating very smelly farts. Beans create large amounts of farts but they are not particularly smelly.

When you smell someone's fart, you are smelling gas made up of atoms and molecules that have been inside them. Perhaps it is best not to think where the atoms have been. Women fart as much as men, and girls fart just as much as boys.

The tongue is the
only muscle in your
body that is only
attached at one
end.

Teeth

Humans have two sets of teeth. The first set of teeth are often called baby teeth, which start growing before a baby is born. The second set of teeth are often called adult teeth and are permanent, so if you lose one it will not be replaced.

Every set of teeth is individual, like a fingerprint. If a dead body is found and no one knows who it is, they can be identified from their dental records.

A third of each tooth is hidden in your gums, so you can only see 2/3 of it. If you have bad gum disease your teeth can fall out - so look after your teeth and gums.

The enamel that coats your teeth is the hardest part of the human body. It has to be hard to protect your teeth.

In the 19th century desperately poor people used to sell their teeth so that they could be used by rich people as false teeth or dentures. False teeth were also made from teeth pulled out of dead bodies on battlefields.

Like fingerprints, every tongue is unique.

Hair

The only places on the outside of your body where hair doesn't grow are the palms of your hands, the soles of your feet and your lips. We have the same number of hairs on our body as a chimpanzee, but most human hairs are thin and almost invisible.

Almost every mammal has hair. Mammals that can be considered hairless include elephants, hippopotamuses and rhinoceroses.

People with red hair have a higher pain threshold than other people, so can withstand pain better than most others can.

Why do boys have nipples?

Boys and men have nipples but they obviously don't serve any purpose, so why have them?

The reason why males have nipples is because nipples are formed when the person is first created in the womb inside their mum's tummy, before nature decides whether the baby is going to be a boy or a girl.

Boys wearing dresses

It was common during Victorian times for little boys to wear dresses until they were 5 or 6.

What is the 'gunk' in your eyes when you wake up?

It is dried mucus (similar to the snot that you get in your nose), dust and dead blood cells.

When you are awake you blink and wash your eyes clean with tears, so the 'gunk' doesn't build up. You blink about 12 times a minute and a blink only lasts a tenth of a second.

The human eye can distinguish about 10 million different colours. If it was a digital camera it would have 576 mega pixels.

What is earwax for?

Earwax stops dust and dust getting into the inner workings of your ear.

Your ears are very delicate and sensitive. Not only are they used for hearing they are also used for balance. Ears have a liquid inside them which enables the brain to know if you are moving or not. When you spin round, it sometimes takes time for the liquid to settle down. This is what happens when you feel dizzy.

When you are asleep your ear keeps working, but your brain shuts out the noise so that you can sleep.

Why can't we tickle ourselves?

When we tickle people, it usually catches people by surprise, but obviously you can't surprise yourself.

Why do we get breathless when we laugh?

Laughing stops people breathing normally, so it is not possible to get air in or air out of your lungs as easily as when you are not laughing.

Facts about babies

A newborn baby has a wee every 20 minutes. When it is six months old it has a wee once an hour.

When a newborn baby cries it can't create tears. It is not until a baby is 3 - 6 weeks old that it can produce tears when it cries.

A baby's head accounts for about a quarter of its body size. In an adult the head accounts for an eighth of the body size.

Babies' eyes can focus most easily at a distance of 25 cm, which is similar to the distance of a mother's breast from a mother's eye.

Babies double their weight in their first six months.

Babies have an incredibly strong grip and can hang in mid-air held by their grip.

When babies are born they don't have kneecaps so they are unable to straighten their legs.

Babies have a natural ability to swim. However they lose this natural ability when they are about six months old.

A mother can feel a baby having hiccups or kicking inside her belly.

The colour of a new born baby's eyes may change a few months after they are born.

There are more germs in the kitchen sink than in your toilet.

A sink typically has around 500,000 bacteria per square inch which is a lot more than in a toilet after it has been flushed.

Body Odour

When people smell it is called body odour or B.O.

What causes body odour? It is caused by sweat.

The body has 3 – 4 million sweat glands that produce sweat. However, sweat doesn't smell, but bacteria love sweat and break down dead skin, creating a smell.

Why are feet often the smelliest part of your body?

Why do feet smell?

Wrapping our feet in shoes and socks creates the ideal environment for the bacteria that produce body odour to thrive. Warm, moist and thick skin on feet is perfect for bacteria. It doesn't help that no air gets to feet to blow away the smell, so when people take their shoes and socks off, feet can be really smelly.

Feet have 250,000 sweat glands which is more sweat glands per square centimetre than anywhere else on the body.

Why does your skin go wrinkly when you have been in the bath for a long time?

When you have been in the bath or swimming pool for a long time your fingers, toes and feet become all wrinkly.

Your skin is covered with a protective layer of special oils that keep your skin waterproof. When you have been soaking in water for a long time the waterproofing is washed away and the outer layer of your skin soaks up water.

The skin on your hands and feet is thicker than the skin elsewhere on the body, so your hands and feet have more dead skin than elsewhere on the body. This means that hands, fingers, feet and toes can soak up more water and become much more wrinkled than skin everywhere else on the body.

Where do our birds go?

Many of Britain's birds spend only part of the year here and travel to other countries for other parts of the year.

Birds that leave in the winter

Swallows escape Britain's cold winter weather every year. In the autumn they gather together in large groups and fly down to southern Africa to spend the winter, a journey of about 9,500 km. Swallows fly 320 km during the day, which is unusual as most migrating birds fly at night. Every spring they make the return journey, travelling through Morocco, Spain and France before arriving back in Britain.

Yellow wagtails and swifts follow a similar route to swallows.

Chiffchaffs spend the winter in the Mediterranean and western Africa, they arrive back in Britain in early spring.

Cuckoos fly to southern Africa. They take a different route from swallows and go through central Europe and Italy before travelling down to sub-Saharan Africa. Willow warblers fly to the west coast of Africa and spend the winter in Ghana and the Ivory Coast.

Seabirds such as puffins and gannets spend the winter months at sea. In the spring they arrive on Britain's coast.

Birds that arrive in the winter

Every winter, birds arrive in Britain to escape the harsh winters in the countries where they spend the summer. Fieldfares come from Scandinavia and Russia, waxwings from Russia's far northern forests, and redwings and bramblings fly south from the north of Britain and north-eastern Europe.

What should you do if you are attacked by a wild animal?

Sharks

If a shark has seen you, the best thing to do is stay calm and avoid sudden movements or panic. Make sure you don't take your eyes off the shark! If the shark is clearly very interested in you, the best thing to do is to swim away quickly and smoothly without causing too much disturbance in the water.

If a shark attacks you, hit it on the nose. If you are swimming in water where you know there is a possibility of shark attack, it is best to have an object with you such as a stick, pole or diving knife.

In the worse case situation when a shark gets you in its jaws, DON'T 'play dead' – defend yourself with all your strength. The shark's eyes and gill openings are good targets to aim for. You must get out of the water as soon as you can.

Most sharks are merely interested in humans and don't attack.

Crocodiles or alligators

The best advice is not to go near alligators or crocodiles. If you think they may be in the water don't go in! If they attack you in a river or in the sea, they may try to drag you down in what is described as a 'death roll' and hold you underwater to drown you. The best course of action is to attack the sensitive parts of the animal: the most sensitive part is the eyes, followed by the nostrils and ears. If you are caught in the jaws of a crocodile or alligator, try and attack the flap of tissue behind its tongue that stops water flowing into its throat, preventing it from drowning when its mouth is open. If you are able to strike this valve, hopefully you will be released and then be able to escape.

If you are being chased on land, run away as fast as possible in a straight line. The advice to run in a zig-zag because the crocodile, with its long body, takes longer to change direction is bad advice. Get as far away as possible as quickly as you can.

Lions and big cats

It is unusual for lions to attack humans. They are more likely to attack if they think their cubs are in danger.

Do not try and run away. Don't turn your back on the animal.

Try to make yourself appear as big as possible, wave your arms, and clap and shout, as this may frighten the animal.

If you are attacked, they will probably go for your face and throat. It is important to try and remain standing. The best advice is to defend yourself by attacking the lion's head and eyes.

Bear attack

The advice here is very general. Different types of bears behave differently so it may well be worth seeking more detailed advice if you know what type of bear you may be attacked by!

Once again, the advice is to make yourself look as big as possible. Back away slowly, speaking in a deep, loud, calm voice, but don't turn your back on the bear. Don't look directly at the bear's eyes.

If a grizzly or polar bear attacks you because it feels threatened, it may be worth 'playing dead', then you will no longer be a threat to the bear.

If a bear is attacking you for non-defensive reasons (it is unlikely that a bear will see you as food, but it is possible) or it is a black bear, DO NOT 'play dead': fight the bear with anything you have to hand. Try fighting it off with a stick and throw anything you can at it (stones, your luggage, camera, pots, pans).

If you have to run away from a bear, remember that they can run very fast and can climb trees. As they move on four paws, they are not so quick at side movements so consider side steps when running away.

Snakes

Only 15% of the world's 3000 snake species are dangerous to humans. There are two different types of snake attack. How can you tell the difference? (Not that you'd want to get close enough to tell!)

Venomous snakes have elliptical pupils; constrictors have round pupils.

Venomous snakes

Venomous snakes kill their prey by poisoning.

When a snake bites, their fangs penetrate the skin and inject the poisonous venom into its prey's body. Some venoms destroy body tissue, some stop the heart beating or stop people breathing, and some cause blood to clot and thicken so that it stops flowing around the body. It is essential to know what type of snake bite you have so that you can get the right treatment (or antidote).

Constriction snakes

Constriction snakes wrap themselves around their prey, crushing it until it stops breathing and dies. The best advice is to remain calm and as still as possible, because heavy breathing and struggling is likely to make the snake increase its grip. If you are right-handed, protect your ribs with your left hand (vice versa if left-handed) and use your right hand to gently unwind the snake. It is difficult to unwind a snake on your own, so without a friend to help it is likely that the snake will succeed!

Britain's only venomous snake is the adder, which is also known as the common viper. It is extremely rare to be bitten by an adder, as they only attack humans when they feel threatened. Adders will normally flee as soon as they sense the ground vibrating when someone walks towards them. An adder bite can cause swelling, make you sick and even cause you to faint. If you are bitten by an adder remain calm, don't run or do anything that will increase your heartbeat as this will speed up the effect of the venom. It is essential to go to a hospital or doctor who will be able to treat the swelling and infection.

Komodo dragons

Komodo dragons are rare animals that are only found in one place in the world, a few islands in Indonesia. They are the world's biggest reptiles and aren't actually dragons at all, but the world's biggest type of lizard, growing up to about 3 metres long.

They use their tongue, which is forked like a snake's, to sniff out food and can smell food up to 4 km away and have sharp, serrated teeth which bite into their prey.

Komodo dragons have deadly poisons within their saliva (spit) which will kill their prey, so if a Komodo dragon bites an animal the spit left on the wound will slowly kill it. Their venom is also lethal.

Dung Beetles

Dung beetles are insects that live off dung, or poo as you might call it. There are thousands of different dung species ranging in size from 1 mm to 6 cm.

They are very strong insects. They can roll dung up to 50 times their weight and can bury dung 250 times their own weight overnight.

Egyptians used to worship and celebrate the scarab beetle, a type of dung beetle.

Flea facts

Fleas are wingless insects that travel by jumping from place to place.

Fleas feed off mammals and birds. They bite and drink the blood of their victim. A female flea can drink 15 times its weight in blood in a day.

Fleas can jump 100 times their own height and have been known to jump over 30 cm.

Why is it difficult to swat a fly?

Flies are able to think very quickly, so when they see something coming towards them or feel the air moving as someone tries to swat them, they are able to decide on their escape route and fly away.

Flies also have compound eyes (about 4,000 lenses in each eye, compared to the 1 lens in each eye that humans have) so they have the ability to see almost a full circle around themselves, so they can easily spot someone trying to swat them.

Flies, like many small animals, see in slow motion? A fly will see a flickering light 7 times faster than a human, so it can react much more quickly.

Eyes on the front animals hunt, eyes on the side animals hide.

Some animals have eyes on the front of their faces, and these are usually expert predators. They are able to judge depth and distance, which is great for tracking and useful for animals like monkeys that swing and leap from tree to tree.

Animals that have eyes on the side of their faces tend to be ones that graze on plants instead of hunting other animals. They have better all-round vision so can spot anything that may attack them. Grazing animals often stick together in large groups, so if one animal spots a predator it can alert all the others.

A crocodile can't
stick its tongue
out.

What is the difference between a crocodile and an alligator?

Generally speaking you might be able to guess, because if you are in America it is more likely to be an alligator and elsewhere it is probably going to be a crocodile. If it is in salt water it will probably be a crocodile as alligators don't live in salt water, however they can tolerate salt water for short periods.

The easiest way to tell the difference is when the jaws are closed tight. The large lower fourth tooth fits into a socket in the upper jaw in an alligator so it cannot be seen, but in a crocodile you can see the large fourth tooth.

What is a mammal?

The animal kingdom is grouped into different types of animal. Mammals are a type of animal.

Mammals are warm blooded, can produce milk to feed their young and have hair or fur.

Humans are mammals.

Whales are also mammals. Whales, dolphins, porpoises, seals, walruses, and many other marine animals are mammals, not fish. The marine mammals exist because about 50 to 60 millions of years ago, some mammals wandered off of the land and into the ocean, where they evolved into different types of marine mammals. For whales and dolphins, their front legs turned into flippers. Their back legs became really tiny, so tiny that you can't even see them when you look at these animals, but they have hind legs still inside their bodies – if you see a skeleton of a whale you can see that it has tiny leg bones near its tail.

What is the difference between an African and an Asian elephant?

The most obvious   difference is that African elephants have much bigger ears than Asian elephants.

But there are other differences between them:

African elephant skin is more wrinkled than Asian elephants'.

African elephants' heads are more rounded than Asian elephants' heads.

African elephants' heads are lower than their shoulders, while Asian elephants' heads are higher than their shoulders.

All African elephants have tusks, only some male Asian elephants have tusks.

African elephants are bigger than Asian elephants.

There are a number of other differences with their tusks, feet and teeth.

Elephants laugh, cry, have incredible memories and can live for more than 70 years.

Apart from the colour what is the difference between a red and a grey squirrel?

Red squirrels are our native squirrels, which means they are naturally at home in Britain. There is evidence that they have been in Britain since the Ice Age 10,000 years ago. Grey squirrels were introduced to Britain less than 150 years ago and came from north America.

Grey squirrels are almost twice the weight of red squirrels, so they eat much more than red squirrels, often leaving the red squirrels without enough food.

Grey squirrels spend most of their time on the ground, on the forest floor. Red squirrels spend most of their time in trees in the forest.

Giraffe facts

Giraffes are the world's tallest land animal with an average height of 5 metres.

They clean out their ears with their long tongues.

When they walk they move both legs on the same side of the body. This way of walking is unique to giraffes but they run in the same way as other animals.

Every giraffe's spots are unique in the same way as fingerprints are unique. As giraffes get older their spots get darker.

Giraffes have exactly the same number of bones in their necks as humans – seven.

Why are horses allowed to poo on the street and dogs aren't?

Horses only eat grass and other plant material, dogs eat meat from a range of animals. It is possible for diseases to be passed on from meat-eating animals to people through poo. Horse poo and poo from other animals that don't eat meat don't have diseases that are dangerous to humans.

Cats have about
20 muscles in each
ear.

When does a kitten become a cat?

Some people say at six months old because they can have kittens themselves at that age, others say at a year old when they stop growing. Some cats stop growing at less than a year old, others continue growing for longer than a year.

Cat live for 12 - 15 years, but some cats live for much longer.

Cats conserve energy by sleeping up to 18 hours a day!

When cats are awake they spend much of their day cleaning their fur by licking it.

Cats have very good night time vision and can see in light that is six times dimmer than a human would need.

Are the cats we have as pets, domestic cats, the only members of the cat family that purr?

Most small cats can purr including wild cats like ocelots and servals. Some larger cats including cheetahs and pumas can also purr.

Big cats can't purr because their throats are designed so that they can roar. Cats that are 'big cats' are lions, tigers, leopards and jaguars.

How can birds fall asleep on tree branches without falling off?

Obviously some birds live in nests in trees, so they don't have to worry about falling out of a tree, but some birds sleep on tree branches.

Some birds have tendons in their feet that tighten and lock the birds' claws onto the branch when they fall asleep.

Banana facts

Where do bananas get their name from?

From the Arabic word for finger which is banan. Bunches of bananas are known as a hand and have ten to twenty fingers.

Almost all the bananas that we eat are descended from a type of banana called the Cavendish banana that was created at Chatsworth House in Derbyshire, England.

Bananas do not grow on trees – the banana plant is the world's largest herb.

Are oranges named after the colour orange, or is the colour orange named after the fruit?

Until oranges were seen in Britain, an old English word that meant 'yellow-red' was used to describe the colour red.

The word orange comes from the old French word 'orenge' which was derived from the Arabic word naranj.

No word rhymes with orange.

Strawberries
are the only fruit
that has seeds
on the outside.
The average
strawberry has
200 seeds.

Pears are the only fruit that ripen from the inside out.

Peanuts

Peanuts are NOT actually nuts, the 'nut' that we eat is a seed that grows underground.

Peanut butter doesn't contain butter. It is only called peanut butter because it is easy to spread on bread and toast.

Sandwiches

Sandwiches were invented by the 4th Earl of Sandwich, who liked to eat a slice of beef between two slices of bread so that he could carry on playing cards while he ate.

Pizza

Where was the first pizza invented and who invented it?

This is one of those questions where some people will argue about what is the correct answer. Most will agree that it was invented in Naples, Italy by the baker Raffaele Esposito in 1889.

However, it is true to claim that food similar to pizza had been enjoyed in a number of Mediterranean countries for centuries.

Dolphins sleep with one eye open.

How do you get out of a maze?

Keep your hand on the left-hand side and keep walking without taking your hand off the side. This is not the quickest way to get through a maze, but you will always find your way out using this method.

What is chocolate made of?

Chocolate is made from cocoa beans, which are the seeds from cocoa trees. The cocoa beans are turned into a liquid and then mixed with milk, sugar and sometimes vegetable fat.

What is the difference between dark chocolate, milk chocolate and white chocolate?

Dark chocolate contains more cocoa than other types of chocolate and is made from cocoa solids and cocoa butter.

Milk chocolate contains fewer cocoa solids and less cocoa butter. It can also be made from milk powder.

White chocolate doesn't contain any cocoa solids but is mainly sugar and milk with a small amount of cocoa butter.

How do you know if an egg has 'gone off'?

If an egg floats it has gone off and shouldn't be eaten.

What came first the chicken or the egg?

Scientists in Sheffield believe the chicken came first, because an egg can only be formed with protein found in chickens. So you had to have chickens before you could have eggs.

Canadian scientists believe eggs came first because dinosaurs were laying eggs before chickens existed.

Make your own mind up!

Why do many children dislike Brussels sprouts?

It is natural for children not to like foods that are bitter because bad food tastes bitter and may be poisonous. Sweet food is generally safe to eat, so children naturally like things that are sweet. Brussels sprouts taste too bitter for many children.

You taste things when food touches the taste buds on your tongue. We can distinguish 5 different tastes: salty, sweet, bitter, sour and umami (which comes from glutamate, like soy sauce). In addition to this, children have roughly twice the number of taste buds on their tongues as adults do and many children have more taste buds that are sensitive to sweet tastes. As you get older, the tastes that you enjoy often change because your taste buds change.

You share your birthday with at least 9 million other people in the world.

Why do trees lose their leaves in winter?

Not all trees lose their leaves. Evergreens and conifers in particular keep their leaves over winter.

Deciduous trees lose their leaves so that the tree can save energy and preserve moisture in its trunk and branches.

As leaves have a high water content, leaves would have problems in freezing weather as they would freeze and be damaged by ice.

Trees only get 10% of the nutrients they need from soil and 90% from the atmosphere. Trees need carbon dioxide, water and sun to grow.

How do trees grow?

Trees grow from the tips of their branches and thicken at their base – so as a tree trunk gets thicker, the branches grow longer and taller.

Why do trees have rings?

Trees grow at different speeds throughout the year. When they are growing quickly the wood is lighter than when they are growing more slowly, and the wood is darker. So we can see rings of different colours.

If there is a cold spell and the tree stops growing during the year, that year might have more than one ring. In areas of the world where the weather is more or less the same every year so that trees grow at the same rate all the time, the trees don't have rings.

Which way does water run down the plug hole?

It depends where you are.

In the southern hemisphere, which is south of the equator, the water flows clockwise, and north of the equator in the northern hemisphere it flows anti-clockwise.

Water is the only substance on earth that is lighter as a solid than it is as a liquid.

Julius Caesar's Last Breath

Every time you take a breath you are breathing in molecules from a famous person from history.

This is usually called the 'Julius Caesar's Last Breath' fact. Every time you breathe you are breathing molecules from the last breath that Julius Caesar took when he died 2,000 years ago.

Everything is made of atoms and molecules. Over time the billions and billions of molecules get mixed up, so the theory is that some of the molecules will still be in the air that you breathe.

It doesn't have to be Julius Caesar's breath, it could be someone else from history, the principle is the same.

How does glue stick?

Glue must have two properties: adhesion so it can stick to the surface it is put on and cohesion so it can bond to the surfaces it is sticking together. For glue to work, it has to bond with both surfaces and stick to itself.

If you make a jam sandwich the jam will stick the bread together. If you peel off both slices of bread you will see that the jam has stuck to both slices. This is an example of how glue works.

How does glue bond with a surface?

Most glues mix with the surface of the material being glued: it seeps into tiny holes too small for the eye to see.

How do washing-up liquid and other cleaners work?

Washing-up liquid is made of molecules that have two ends: one end sticks to the grease and dirt, the other end sticks to the water in the washing-up bowl.

When washing clothes, the washing soap or detergent has a chemical, one end of which attaches to the dirt, the other end to water. When clothes have been soaking in soapy water they can be rinsed clean since the dirt is now floating in the water.

Cleaners may also have a property that scientists call a 'wetting agent'. This is a chemical that breaks the grip of dirt particles so that they can be washed away.

Why is the sky blue?

The light from the sun is made up of many different colours. This is called the spectrum. When blue light hits dust and water droplets in the sky it is reflected and bounced all over the sky, while other colours in the spectrum carry on shining down to earth. On a very sunny day, the sky is really blue because there is a lot of blue light reflecting around the sky.

Why are sunsets red?

As the sun is setting, just before it goes out of view, it is less bright and appears red.

This is because only the red colours in the spectrum can be seen, since the other colours in the spectrum have been absorbed by the sky or scattered.

What is a supermoon?

The distance between the earth and the moon varies, so that sometimes the moon is closer to earth.

When a full moon falls at the same time as the moon is closer to earth, it is called a supermoon because the moon appears to be bigger and brighter.

The Earth is 93 million miles away from the sun.

So if you can see the sun, you can see something 93 million miles away!

Why are there 365 days in a calendar year?

This is the time it takes for the earth to go round the sun.

BUT other planets' years are different: some are longer than an earth year and some are shorter.

Mercury	87.96	Earth days
Venus	224.6	Earth days
Mars	686.98	Earth days
Jupiter	11,862	Earth years
Saturn	29,456	Earth years
Uranus	84.07	Earth years
Neptune	247.7	Earth years

How long is a day?

A day is the time it takes for a planet to turn round one complete circle.

It takes the earth 24 hours to spin round one complete circle.

A day on Jupiter is only 9.8 hours.

A day on Venus is longer than a year on Venus. It takes 243 Earth days for Venus to spin round a full circle, but it takes 224.7 Earth days for Venus to circle the sun.

Why is Easter at a different time every year?

Christmas is always on the 25th December so why does the date of Easter change every year?

It is based on the lunar calendar, which is based on the moon. The general rule is that Easter Sunday is the first Sunday following the first full moon after the 21st March.

Big Ben is the name of the bell in the tower at the Palace of Westminster also known as the Houses of Parliament.

Many people think it is the name of the clock or the name of the tower.

The British Parliament is sometimes called the 'Mother of Parliaments' – but it wasn't the first parliament. Greece probably had the first parliament.

The oldest parliament is in Iceland, the Althing dates from 930 A.D.

The oldest continuous parliament is in the Isle of Man which began in 979 A.D.

What is Greenwich Mean Time?

Greenwich Mean Time (GMT) became the world's time standard from which all other times would be set in 1884. It has been renamed as Universal Time, which is sometimes shortened to UT.

During British Summer Time (BST) in the summer, clocks go forward one hour which means we have more daylight in the evening.

Why does the world have different time zones?

The sun rises at different times in different places as the earth rotates.

Different parts of the world are in different time zones, so that people can make best use of the daylight every day. When the sun is at its highest point, it is generally the middle of the day.

What Do Place Names Mean?

A place name can often tell you about the history of a place. Many British place names are links to history and use Roman, Viking or Anglo-Saxon words to describe a place.

Place names which include 'chester' often mean that the place was the site of a Roman military camp or fort which would have been called a 'castra'. Sometimes the word 'castra' has become -caster or -cester.

Sussex, Essex, Wessex and Middlesex are all names derived from when England was ruled by the Saxons after the Romans had left. Wessex was West Saxons, Sussex was South Saxons, Essex was East Saxons and Middlesex was the central or middle Saxon area.

Many place names are related to the name of the river running through the village, town or city or the river crossing. Obviously if the river was crossed by a bridge, the place name would include the word bridge.

If the river was crossed by a ford – a shallow river crossing that people could walk through – ford would be included in the name.

It is sometimes easy to guess why a place has got its name. Obviously market is because the place had a market, mouth is found at the coast where a river reaches the sea, and field suggests that the place was originally a field!

Longest place name

Llanfairpwllgwyngyllgogerychwyrndrobwllllanty-siliogogogoch is the longest place name in the United Kingdom. As you can probably guess it is in Wales.

In English the name means, St Mary's Church in the hollow of the white hazel near to the rapid whirlpool of Llantysilio of the red cave.

Newtown is the most popular name for a British town. Over 150 towns are named Newtown.

Where do surnames come from?

Surnames are passed on from generation to generation, so someone's surname may suggest their family roots. If someone has an eastern European name they probably have ancestors from eastern Europe, similarly a surname can be linked to countries and cultures from Asia, Africa or anywhere in the world.

Most traditional British surnames fall into various categories. Some tell you about their occupation, for example Taylor. Others are family relationships, e.g. the son of someone, such as Stevenson. Place names may describe where people lived, for example Hill, while some surnames have been created from a description of a person's character or appearance, such as Smart.

There are over 30,000 people with the name John Smith in Britain.

Why are the Royal Family the Windsors?

The Royal Family changed their surname from Saxe-Coburg-Gotha to Windsor. The change took place in 1917 during the first World War when it was decided it was best not to have a German surname when Britain was at war with Germany. George V decided to name the family after one of the royal castles.

The name Wendy was made up for the book Peter Pan.

Road crossings

A Belisha beacon is a light in an orange ball on the top of a black and white striped pole that flashes. They are named after Leslie Hore-Belisha who introduced them to Britain in the 1930s.

Zebra crossings, which were introduced in the 1950s, are thick black and white stripes on the road, to let drivers know that they should stop and let people cross the road.

A Pelican crossing is a crossing where the lights are controlled by people pressing a button. The name was created from the description PEdestrian LIght-CoNtrolled crossing. It was decided to call it after an animal after the success of the Zebra crossing.

Puffin crossings: this name comes from Pedestrian User Friendly Intelligent CrossiNg. These are set diagonally to the road edge so that people can watch the traffic carefully whilst waiting for the signal to cross.

Traffic lights were invented before cars. The first traffic lights were close to the Houses of Parliament in London. They only had red for stop and green for go, and were used to control horse-drawn traffic and pedestrians. They used to use gas instead of electricity, but when they blew up and killed a policeman this idea was dropped.

The first traffic lights for cars were introduced in New York in 1918 and in Britain at a busy junction near London's Piccadilly in 1925. Britain's first automatic traffic lights which did not need to be operated by a policeman were installed in Wolverhampton in 1926.

Is it true that the tin opener was invented many years after the tin was invented?

Often there is more than one person who can claim to have invented something or be the first person to make a discovery.

Some believe that cans are a French invention because Nicolas Appert won a prize from the French military leader Napoleon for 'canned heat-preserved food' before the tin can was invented by a Londoner, Peter Durand.

For nearly 50 years before can openers were invented people had to open cans with a hammer and chisel. Some people believe that the can opener was invented by the Englishman Robert Yates in 1855. The American Ezra Warner also claimed to be the inventor with his 1858 can opener.

The temperature scale used to be the other way round!

The Swedish scientist Anders Celsius invented the Celsius temperature scale. This is now often called degrees C or centigrade because he designed his scale so there would be 100 units or increments between the temperature at which water freezes and the temperature at which it boils. Originally in 1742, 100° was freezing and 0° was boiling point, but two years later in 1744 after buying his first thermometer he reversed the scale.

What is the best thing to do if stuck in a bog or quicksand?

1 First: don't panic. Rapid movement might drag you further down into the bog or quicksand.

2 Take time to assess the situation. Is there anyone who can help? Is there anything you can grab on to? What is the best direction to take? How deep are you in: down to your knees, waist, chest or further?

3 Slowly try to free one leg.

4 If you are close to waist deep, it is important to increase the amount of your surface that is in contact with the bog. Try to lie on top of the bog, and then hopefully you can roll and snake out of it.

5 If the bog or quicksand is watery, make movements as if you were swimming breast stroke slowly.

6 If you avoid panicking and make a slow, calm escape, you will be fine.

How do you navigate without a compass?

Use the sun. If it is the morning the sun will be in the east, and if it is the afternoon it will be in the west.

How did sailors navigate before compasses were invented?

Sailors used the sun, stars and basic charts to navigate.

In the early days of sailing, sailors believed the earth was flat and they could sail off the end of the earth!

What did people wipe their bottoms with before toilet roll?

The Romans used to use a sponge on a stick – they also had communal toilets where they would sit in a row and water would flow in a channel below to wash everything away.

Many people in history have used leaves and grass – in some parts of the world where they don't have toilet roll they still use leaves and grass.

In the past (and in some countries and cultures people still do this) people used their left hand and then washed their hand in running water. This is why it is good manners to shake hands with your right hand, not your left hand.

When did people start wearing underwear?

In ancient history people used to wear loincloths. Think of Tarzan or a loose fitting nappy made from animal skin and you will have the right idea.

In the 13th century men used to wear braies, which were similar to shorts.

Women started wearing 'draws' at the start of the 19th century, consisting of two legs with a cord that was used to tie them together. Only rich women wore draws.

At the end of the 19th century women started wearing knickers.

Why do women's clothes button the other way round from men's clothes?

Women's clothing is buttoned right over left, and men's clothing is buttoned left over right.

This dates from the time when women were dressed by personal maids, so the buttons were arranged to make it easier for the maids.

Football

Football is the most played and most watched sport on Earth. The only countries that call football soccer are the U.S.A. and Canada.

The oldest football club in the world is Sheffield F.C., formed in 1857, but none of the football clubs formed before 1857 exist any more. The first FA Cup took place in 1872.

Before crossbars were introduced in 1882, so long as the ball went between the goalposts it counted as a goal. In the 1890s nets were introduced to goals as people were tired of wasting time collecting the ball after a goal. Referees only started using whistles in 1878, so before 1878 it is believed that they used to wave a white handkerchief or flags or just had to shout as loud as they could.

Why do we bowl overarm in cricket?

In the 18th century cricket was a popular game for women to play, and there is evidence that women have played cricket since the game first started. In the early 19th century women started bowling overarm because otherwise their wide skirts got in the way. Overarm bowling became part of cricket rules in 1964, which some people regard as the birth of modern cricket.

Why is the length of a cricket pitch 22 yards?

The distance of 22 yards, which 20.12 metres, is the only rule in cricket that has remained unchanged throughout the history of the game. The distance is a chain, an old English unit of measurement created in 1620.

Cricket is the second most popular sport in the world and is played in over 130 countries.

Bicycles

Bicycles are considered to be the most efficient method of transport.

Nearly 98 % of the energy used to ride a bike is converted into forward movement. If a car was as efficient as a bicycle it would go for 1,600 miles on a gallon of petrol.

Britain's Security Service

What does MI stand for in MI5 and MI6?

The MI stands for Military Intelligence and the number stands for the department.

MI5 deals with threats from within the UK and MI6 is the Secret Intelligence Service and deals with threats from outside the UK.

During WWII there were once many different Military Intelligence agencies. Other agency numbers include MI9 Undercover Operations, MI1 Code Breaking and MI4 Aerial Reconnaissance.

Were Cinderella's party shoes really made of glass?

The fairy tale of Cinderella is hundreds of years old and there are many versions of the story, with a Chinese version which is over a thousand years old. In different versions of the Cinderella story, set in many countries at different times in history, Cinderella's shoes were made out of different materials. In one version her shoes were made of fur.

It is believed that the first time Cinderella's shoes were made out of glass was in a French version written in the 17th Century nearly four hundred years ago.

Why do animals eat their own poo?

There are quite a lot of animals that eat their own poo: rabbits, gorillas, many insects and even dogs!

Rodents and rabbits will eat their own poo because a diet of plants and vegetables is hard to digest. Other animals eat their own poo because it is full of nutrients and good for them!

Why do we give the thumbs-up sign?

The thumbs-up gesture is used to wish good luck or agreement.

Whilst we don't know for certain, the most popular explanation is that it dates back to Roman times. A thumbs-up signal would indicate that a gladiator would be spared and could live. The thumbs-down signal would indicate that the gladiator would be fed to the lions.

However, there are records that suggest that when the crowd gave the thumbs-up signal they thought the gladiator should be sent to face the lions and certain death. Perhaps they enjoyed seeing gladiators being sent to the lions?

Why do we cross our fingers for luck?

Nobody knows for certain. Crossing fingers for luck is a superstition that is mainly found in Christian countries. During Roman times when Christians were persecuted by Romans, Christians used to show their crossed fingers to recognise each other.

In 16th century England crossing fingers was seen as a way of protecting against evil, people also crossed their fingers when people sneezed or coughed.

What did the Romans give Britain?

Before the Romans, the Celts lived in Britain. The country had many different tribes ruled by many different kings and chiefs. There were no towns, most people were farmers and lived in villages.

The calendar

Roman leader Julius Caesar developed the Roman calendar and created the Julian calendar which is the calendar that we still use today.

Towns

The Romans built towns across the country. Many of the towns still exist and have grown to become cities.

Indoor plumbing

The Romans brought running water inside buildings. They created huge baths in public buildings so people could have baths together.

Straight roads and paved streets

You can often tell if a modern road follows the path of a Roman road because it is straight. The Romans built straight roads because they knew it was the shortest distance between two places.

Roman roads were carefully constructed with foundations. They sloped towards the middle so that water could run away, and were paved with stones so that they had a strong surface.

Rabbits

We know that rabbits were brought to Britain by the Romans, as rabbit remains have been found with remains of Roman pottery.

Bricks and cement

The first buildings built in Britain using bricks and cement were built by the Romans.

The Anglo-Saxons ruled Britain after the Romans, so did the Anglo-Saxons fight the Romans?

When the Anglo-Saxons came to power the Romans had more or less left Britain, so the Anglo-Saxons didn't have to fight the Romans. The Anglo-Saxons ruled for over 600 years until the Normans invaded from France.

What was William the Conqueror's real name?

At school we are taught that William the Conqueror was the last person to successfully invade Britain, but his name wasn't William. He is considered to be the first Norman king, he came from France and as everyone knows won the Battle of Hastings.

On his tomb his name is written Guillelmus, the Norman French didn't have a letter 'W' in their alphabet, so the English changed the 'Guil' sound to 'Will' similar to the German spelling of the sound. Before long this name became William and for hundreds of years it has been one of Britain's most popular names.

Why is Great Britain called Great Britain?

We don't have Great France, Great Spain or 'Great' other countries so why do we have Great Britain?

The name Great Britain came about in medieval times to distinguish the country from Brittany when Brittany was called Petite Bretagne (Little Britain).

When Britain's parliament signed the Act of Union in 1880 with Ireland's parliament, the United Kingdom was formed.

Stamps

Britain was the first country to use postage stamps and is the only country in the world that doesn't have the country name on its stamps.

Before postage stamps were invented, people had to pay the postman when the letter was delivered.

When stamps were first made, people had to use glue to stick them on.

Why do we drive on the left in Britain?

It dates back to the days when people used to carry swords when travelling around the country. They would pass each other on the left, so that the other person would be on their right-hand side. Their swords would be kept on their left-hand side, so they would be able draw their sword with their right hand should the need arise.

Armies marched on the left, which is believed to date from Roman times.

Why does Europe drive on the right?

Since Napoleon was left-handed and therefore drew his sword the opposite way from right-handers, he decided that the French army would march on the right, and imposed this rule on all the countries that he conquered.

Who invented the equals symbol?

Everyone is used to using the = to mean equals when doing maths, but not everyone knows that the symbol was invented by Robert Recorde, who lived in Tenby in south Wales. Apparently he got tired of writing the word 'equals' so invented the symbol.

If you add up the opposite sides of a dice it will always equal 7.

Who invented the word 'hello'?

Most words haven't been invented, many have developed over time. The word 'hello' was invented by American Thomas Edison who is one of the people credited with inventing the telephone. Previously the word 'hullo' was used, but the first person to have spelt and used the word 'hello' was Edison who thought it was a good word to start a telephone conversation.

Apparently the women who worked as telephone operators (connecting people in the days before it was possible to connect to telephones by dialling) were known as 'hello girls'.

Why do animals hibernate?

Hibernation is when animals go to sleep for the winter.

Hibernation enables animals to survive when there is limited food to eat. Before hibernating many animals eat a lot of food to build up fat reserves. When hibernating animals are in a deep sleep, their heart rate slows so that they don't use up much energy.

Where does the expression 'saved by the bell' come from?

We can't be certain of the origin of the phrase. Many people believe it comes from boxing, when a boxer instead of being beaten gets a chance to recover because the bell is rung to mark the end of a round.

However, some believe it may well be from a time when medical science was not as advanced as it is today. People were worried that they might think they were dead, but might actually still be alive.

People used to tie a string to the hand or foot of a dead body and attach it to a bell. If the bell rang, the body would be dug up and the person would be saved by the bell.

Where does the expression 'bless you' come from?

Before we had modern medicine and the plague, infectious diseases might kill people. A cold would be seen as something to worry about, as it could be the first sign of an infection. By saying 'bless you' the person was asking God to help keep you well.

Where does the expression 'not enough room to swing a cat' come from?

The expression dates back to the early days of the navy and is nothing to do with our furry pets. The cat that the saying refers to is a cat o' nine tails, which was a whip. The whip had nine 'tails' so whipping the victim meant nine strokes with every lashing. To use the whip needed space, so in a small space sailors used to say that 'there was not enough room to swing a cat'.

What does the expression 'over a barrel' mean and where does it come from?

The expression means that you are in a situation where you have little or no choice.

There are various explanations of possible sources for this expression, mainly involving barrels and punishment. One suggestion is that people were tied to barrels so that they couldn't escape and punished. It is suggested that the barrel in question might be the barrel of a cannon. What we do know is that being 'over a barrel' is not a good position to be in.

Where does the expression 'a stitch in time saves nine' come from'?

This is used to mean that it is best to do something when it only needs a small amount of work, rather than waiting until later when the situation has got worse.

It is not known exactly when the expression was first used, but it is mentioned in a book published in 1732.

What does it mean when people say that something passes the 'acid test' and where does the expression come from?

To say that something passes the acid test means that you can be certain.

The expression comes from America during the gold rush. When people thought they had found a piece of gold, a sample was tested in acid and if it didn't dissolve it passed the test.

When it is cold some people say it is 'cold enough to freeze the balls off a brass monkey'?

Where does the expression come from?

Many people believe it comes from the days of cannonballs on navy ships. A brass monkey was a rack that stored cannonballs. When it was cold the steel cannonballs would fall through the brass monkey because they shrank in cold weather.

Why are children better than adults?

Children have better hearing than adults, so they can hear higher notes.

Children have more bones than adults. Babies have about 300 bones but as people grow up their bones fuse together, so adults only have just over 200 bones.

Children are better at learning languages.

Children laugh more than adults.

Children are better at making friends than adults.

Children are better at asking questions.

Children don't smell as much as adults, as they don't have as many active sweat glands.

Children are happier than adults.